FWOFF
OOH! SKY-FISH.
YOU CAN SEE THE TOWER REAL CLEAR TODAY...
PERFECT DAY FOR A *LIFT*—!

Psalms of Planet Eureka seveN
by BONES
Comics by Jinsei Kataoka, Kazuma Kondou
© 2005 BONES / Project EUREKA–MBS

HOHH.
TMP
TMP
HAHH.
YOH!
TOMP
HAHH.
WAH!
ZLIPP
ZLUMP
~~~CRAP.
ZOPP
~~~

RENTON THURSTON... AGE 14.
Right, then.
Yoh.
FWOFF
I DO TODAY WHAT I DO *EVERY* DAY—GO *LIFT* ON THE *TRAPAR* AT THE BOTTOM OF THE CLIFF.
GWOOSH
YEAH!

THERE'S NOTHING LIKE THE WIND IN YOUR FACE...
TRAPAR'S *INVISIBLE*, SO IT REALLY IS LIKE FLOATING IN THIN AIR.
IT'S *AWESOME*, RIDING A TRAPAR-WAVE.
THE REST OF IT...?

IT *SUCKS*.

Y'KNOW
?
PEACE
SURE IS
A PAIN IN
THE BUTT.
SUBURBS OF
BELLE FOREST

KLATT
THE "SUMMER OF LOVE"...
...ALSO KNOWN AS THE WORST TRAGEDY IN OUR HISTORY.
DUE TO UNUSUALLY HIGH CONCENTRATIONS OF TRAPAR IN OUR SKIES, COMMUNICATIONS AND OTHER TRANSMISSIONS CONNECTING THE TOWERS WERE SEVERELY DISRUPTED.
パラ...
FLIP...
AS FOR THE HERO WHO CAME FORTH DURING THAT TIME OF NEED...

GEKKO 5-10
ADROCK-THURSTON
TOPIC 94
SUMMER OF LOVE
NEW COLOR!
...THAT, OF COURSE, WOULD BE ADROCK THURSTON.
IN OTHER WORDS, MY DAD.
HEY, RENTON...
DID ANYONE ACTUALLY SEE IT...?
HE DID SUPPOSEDLY SAVE THE WORLD, SO...
HEY, I BARELY EVEN REMEMBER WHAT HE LOOKED LIKE.
It's just...
YOU DON'T REALLY SEEM THE "SON-OF-A-HERO" TYPE TO ME, IS ALL.
HWAHN ?!

...YOU'RE NOT THE ONLY ONE.
HERE'S THE THING: EVEN I DON'T—
NO TALKING IN CLASS!

VOCATIONAL GUIDANCE COUNSELOR
SLAM!
RENTON GOES TO MILITARY SCHOOL OVER MY DEAD BODY!!
WE'RE JUNKMEN, YOU GOT THAT?!

THERE'S, AH...NOT MUCH CHANCE OF THAT, NOT WITH THESE GRADES.
NO CHANCE, IN FACT.

B-BEING THE SON OF THE GREAT ADROCK, WE WOULD OF COURSE PREFER THAT HE...

YEAH?! WHAT I'D PREFER IS FOR THE MILITARY TO GO AND-!
WH-WHICH IS WHAT I...
MR. THURSTON, PLEASE!!
GAARR
Sigh
SOLDIER... JUNKMAN... HERO'S SON- SO MANY ROLES...

...BUT DOES ANYONE BOTHER ASKING ME...??
FORGET ALL OF `EM.
KLUMPK

ray=out 10
MAGAZINE
IF ONLY I COULD RIDE A LIFT BOARD LIKE *HOLLAND*...
HOW COOL WOULD THAT BE...?
...YEAH. AS *IF*.
BEING *BORN* IN THIS STUPID TOWN WASN'T BAD ENOUGH...
HOW MUCH YOU WANNA BET I *DIE* HERE, TOO?!
KEEP OUT
ation!
not enter here
he permission
a military ground.

—WHOA!
HEY, KID! YOU'RE NOT S'PPOSED TO *BE* HERE...
BUT... THIS IS WHERE...I ALWAYS...
GAH!
AH! YOU MUST BE A *LIFTER* ...
LEMME GUESS— THAT REBEL WANNABE *HOLLAND* GOT YOU INTO IT, AM I RIGHT??
THIS *TRAPAR* SPOT'S OFF-LIMITS TO YOU NOW...
THE MILITARY'S GONNA BE BUILDIN' A *BASE* HERE SOON.

LIKE I SAID BEFORE...

PEACE SUCKS.

HOH-H-H
BAH
BAH
BAH
BAH
BAH
GWOHH
ZWAH
ZOOH

THREE OF US AND WE *STILL* CAN'T HIT—!
IT'S TOO FAST...!
IT'S HEADIN' DOWN... AFTER IT!!
!?
LOST
WHERE THE HELL'S HIS LFO?!
STOP WITH THE MISSILES, ALREADY...
THE SKY'S CLUTTERED ENOUGH.

WHAT THE— ?!

SKATTA

...BUT THEN, HOLLAND, THAT'S YOU...
KLIK!
KLIK!
...SECOND-COMING OF THE HERO ADROCK.

909 HOLLAND HERE...
ENEMY RECON DESTROY-ED.
TIME TO SEND HER OUT IN THE NIRVASH...
MOON-LIGHT, ROGER.
BWEE
606 MATTHIEU, O.K.!
...LET'S GET OUT OF HERE.
SO THAT *CRAZY OLD HERMIT* IS STILL...
SP
SPARK
SPARK

EVENIN'!
OH! HELLO THERE.
GUESS WHO'S DUG UP THREE RIGS SUITABLE FOR A LARGE LFO...?
HEH, HEH
YEAH, HUH?
YA-A-AWN
GLONK
DYEH?!
RENTON! PULL YOUR THUMB OUT OF YOUR ASS.
YOU AND THAT GUSSIED-UP PIECE A' PLANK...!
Pff!
IT'S *NOT* A PLANK—!
Oww...
IT'S A *REFLECTION BOARD!*
GEKKOSTATE
IT RIDES ON WAVES OF *TRAPAR*...

......
WAVES I WISH WOULD TAKE ME THE HECK *OUTTA* HERE.

FEH!
YOU'RE JUST STAR-STRUCK BY THAT FAKE-HERO *HOLLAND*, IS ALL...
!
YOU SHUT UP ABOUT HOL-LAND!!
YOU THINK HE LEFT THE MILITARY AND BECAME A GUERILLA BECAUSE IT WAS *FUN*...?!
NOT EVERYONE'S GOT *PEACE* ON THE BRAIN LIKE *YOU* ALL THE TIME-!
BAM!

AND I SUPPOSE YOU *DON'T*, RENTON...?
WHAT'S ON *YOUR* BRAIN—NOT BEING A *HERO*, I HOPE...??

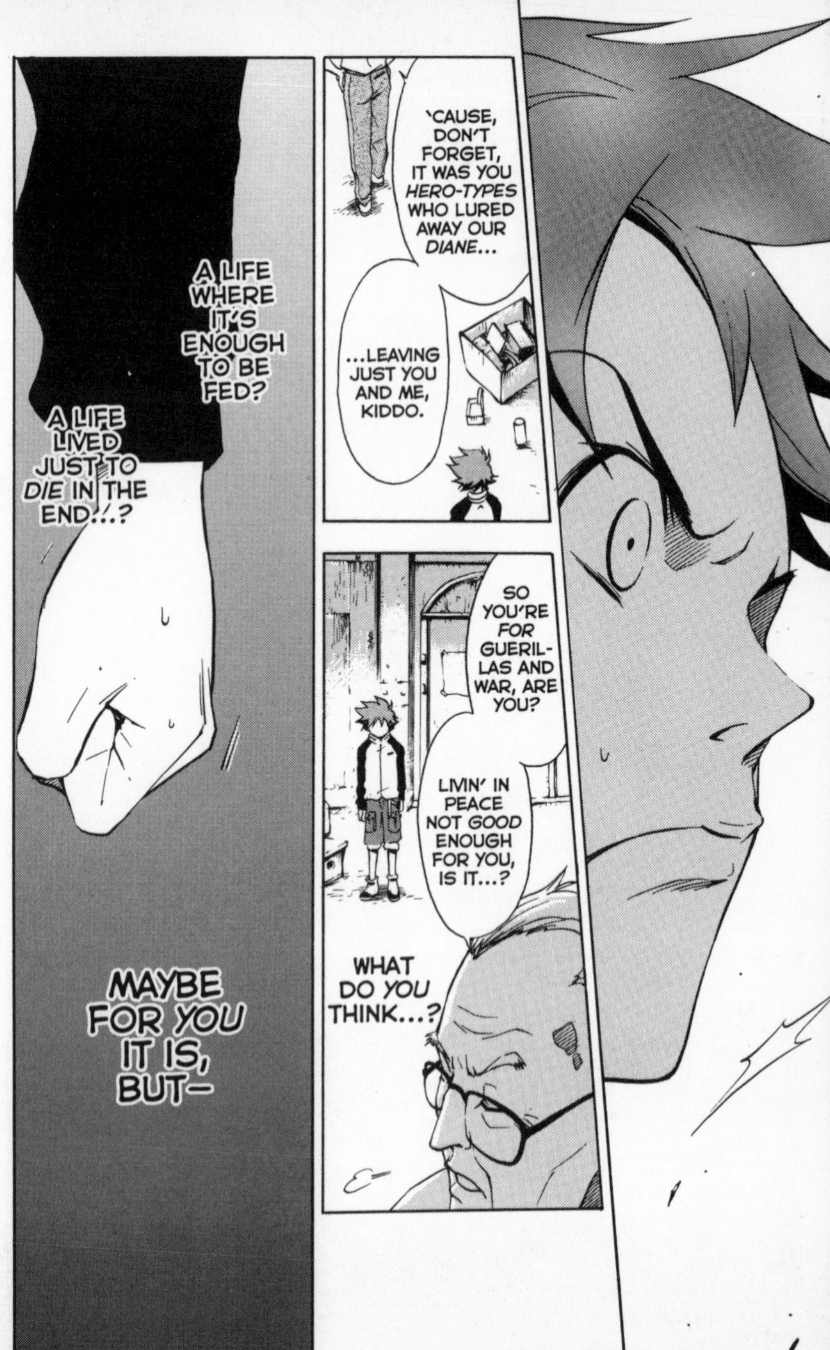
'CAUSE, DON'T FORGET, IT WAS YOU *HERO-TYPES* WHO LURED AWAY OUR *DIANE*...
...LEAVING JUST YOU AND ME, KIDDO.
SO YOU'RE *FOR* GUERIL-LAS AND WAR, ARE YOU?
LIVIN' IN PEACE NOT *GOOD* ENOUGH FOR YOU, IS IT...?
WHAT DO *YOU* THINK...?
A LIFE WHERE IT'S ENOUGH TO BE FED?
A LIFE LIVED JUST TO *DIE* IN THE END...?
MAYBE FOR *YOU* IT IS, BUT—

...WHAT. SPIT IT OUT.
...'S NOTHING.
......
...AD-ROCK...

DIANE'S GONE FOR GOOD...

DO YOU HAVE TO TAKE *RENTON*, TOO?

...IF ONLY YOU'D NEVER *FOUND* THIS.

I SEE NOW, DIANE...
...WHY IT IS YOU COULDN'T WAIT TO *LEAVE*.
FWUMP
BONES
....
WHAT *WAVES* WILL I EVER CATCH STAYING *HERE*...?
GRUMM
GRUMM
GRUM
RUMM
GRUMM...
GROMP

KRAAASH

PSHOOM
WH...
WHAT THE ...?
KOFF
BUT THAT'S ...
...AN LFO, ISN'T IT?!
NOT THAT I'VE EVER SEEN ONE QUITE LIKE–
WHAT IS IT...??
BWEEN
Dwah?
HEY! YOU! PILOT!!
WHAT TH' HECK D'YOU THINK YOU'RE ...

SEE?
STILL HALF-ASLEEP, THIS ONE.

YOU *DO* KNOW ABOUT WAKING, DON'T YOU?
OH MAN, IS SHE...

CUTE!!!

...OH, MAN.

SHE CALLS *THAT* A LANDING?!

THE ENEMY MUST KNOW OUR LOCATION FOR *SURE*.

THAT OLD JUNKYARD CAN'T *REEEALLY* FIX THE NIRVASH, CAN IT??

WHY DIDN'T YOU GO *YOURSELF* IF IT COULD—?

THE WORLD'S FIRST HUMANOID, MOBILE MACHINE, LFO...*

...THE *TYPE ZERO*, PROTOTYPE FOR ALL THAT WOULD COME AFTER...

...FINAL, MISSING PIECE OF THE NIRVASH—!

*LFO = [L]ight [F]inding [O]peration

HEY...

THERE'S NO *COMPACT DRIVE* IN HERE!

IT WON'T WORK WITHOUT IT, YOU KNOW!

WHERE'S IT MOVED TO?

IT HASN'T.

NIRVASH HAS NO NEED OF ONE.

AN LFO WITH-OUT A COMPACT DRIVE...?
Huh!
NO.
WHAT NEED, WHEN THERE'S A PURE HEART...?
....
I, uh...
YOU'RE...
KINDA STRANGE, AREN'T YOU.
...HOLLAND SAID, IF WE WERE TO COME HERE, THIS ONE MIGHT BE REPAIRED.
!!
Y-YOU...
YOU DON'T ACTUALLY KNOW HOLLAND, DO YOU??
?
THEN YOU KNOW OF HIM?

KNOW OF HIM? ARE YOU *KIDDING*?!

THE GREAT HERO WHO TURNED HIS BACK ON THE MILITARY AND FOUNDED THE GEKKO STATE?

THE INSURGENT WHO FIGHTS HIS NEVER-ENDING BATTLE, WHILE RIDING THE WAVES ON *LIFT* SPOTS AROUND THE GLOBE...?

OF *COURSE* I KNOW HIM—HE'S *MY IDOL!*

ray=out

WANTED

HOLAND

See??

I EVEN HAVE A GEKKO DECAL RIGHT *HERE!*

So you do.

... RIGHT, THEN!

THIS CHANGES *EVERYTHING!*

....

*Also known as the The United Federation Forces of Predgio Towers
UPF IZUMO BATTA-LION MS 20 HERE...*
THE TARGET'S BEEN LOCATED.
ROGER THAT.
DRAW THEM OUT.
—UNDER-STOOD.

RATTLE
RATTLE
SO.
Huh.
THE COMPACT DRIVE REALLY DOESN'T SEEM TO HELP...
DWOM
!!

ARE YOU DONE FIXING?
......!!!
N-NOT YET, NO. B-BUT I'M ALMOST ...
LET'S HAVE A LOOK AT...
B-BMP
B-BMP
H-HER HAIR...
IT SMELLS SO GOOD, SO MUCH LIKE–
B-BMP
!
ばっ
BWAH
......

BWEE BWEEE
......!
SHAKE
SHAKE
!?
WHAT TH'–?!
THEY'RE HERE!
...EEEE...
DWAH?!
DOOM
ZWAH
ZOOM

KOFF
KOFF
WH... WHAT TH' HECK IS IT THIS TIME...?!
GWOH
.....!
ALL THOSE MILITARY LFOs...!

GWOH
GWOH
DOMP

SWITCH

BWEEN...

CLOMP

STOMP!

WHERE D'YOU THINK *YOU'RE* GOING...?!

IT'S NOT REPAIRED YET! I STILL HAVEN'T–

YOU'LL HAVE TO COME, TOO.

I-I WANNA *HELP* YOU, OF COURSE, BUT...

B-BMP

AND I *DO* WANNA BOARD AN LFO, BUT...

B-BMP

I-I'M NOT *READY* TO GO UP AGAINST THE...

I-I MEAN, THE *MILITARY* IS...

I-IT'S ALL HAPPENING SO *FAST*, AND...

B-BMP

......?

YOU SAY YOU DO, AND YET DON'T...?
B-BUMP
I'M NOT THE ONLY ONE WHO'S "STRANGE."

THRUS-S-ST
....
I...
...I...
AND YOU'RE OKAY WITH THIS.
THIS IS...
...OKAY WITH YOU.

......!

ACTUALLY, NO-!
DASH!
IT'S NOT OKAY-!!

KLATTA
LIFT
KICK!
VRUM
VRUM
GRIP!
VRUMM
-REN-TON!

SO YOU'RE ACTUALLY *GOING*, ARE YOU?
STEP
GRAND-PA...
I...
-HERE. GOING-AWAY PRESENT.
CATCH
!
HUH?
IT'S WHAT YOU'LL NEED TO COMPLETE **NIRVASH.**
!

FEH.
TAP
SKATTA
GO AND PLAY HERO, THEN, IF YOU MUST.
...I WILL!
ALL THIS TIME...
VROM-M-M
...WAITING FOR THAT WAVE.

!?
EVEN IF A WAVE DOES COME...
HEY! YOU ON THE BIKE! WHERE D'YOU THINK YOU'RE-?!
VROO-
OO
......!?
DID YOU HEAR ME?! THIS IS A MILITARY INSTALLA-
-OOM
HEY! DID YOU HEAR WHAT I-?!
IF YOU'RE TOO SCARED TO CATCH IT...
KEEPOUT
KEEPOUT
!

IT MAY AS WELL NOT EVEN COME!!
BRAKK
KEER
UT
BOMPH
BOMPH
STAGGER...
HFF
HFF
!

YAH
HHHHHH
BKOMPH

I'M IN LOVE WITH YOU—

....
DID I JUST...?
fwump
OHMY-GO... I-I DIDN'T MEAN ...!
I-I MEAN, I DID, BUT...
BWUMP
Uwaa-a-ah!
......
INSIDE VOICE, INSIDE VOICE...!
A-AS FOR WHY I...
...WHY I'VE COME...
SHUFF
...IT'S TO GIVE NIRVASH A PROPER WAKING-UPPING!!
KATCH

SO HOW 'BOUT IT...?
!
...!!
BOMPH
BOMPH
BOMPH

BWAH
UWA-
A-
AH!
SHAKE
RATTLE
THWOMP
ROLL
!
HEY... SNAP OUT'VE IT!
HEY!!
SLUMP...

MOON-LIGHT HERE...
IT WHAT?!
THAT LAST MILITARY ATTACK'S GOT NIRVASH DOWN 97%...!
AT THIS RATE, ANY SECOND NOW...
...IT'S GONNA HIT GROUND—HARD!!

SLAM
BOMP!
BANG
THIS IS BAD—REALLY, *REALLY* BAD!
THE ENEMY!
THE GROUND—!!
BANG
THWOMP
GRAB
UWAAAAAAA
SHWOOOOOSH
NUH-UNH!
SQUEEZE
NO *WAY* DO I DIE HERE...!!

I'VE JUST STARTED T' *LIVE* ...!
BWOMM
BEEP
I...
E
I ONLY JUST *CAUGHT* THIS WAVE—!!
EURE
BEEP
WORK...
WORK, DAMN YOU—!!

DAMMIT, NIRVASH...
WAKE UP!!

FLASH!
EUREKA

GLINT
EUREKA
......!?
"EH-OOH..."
"EH-OOH-WRECK-AH"...?

ZWASSH
HOL-LAND! WHAT'S THIS LIGHT?!
...WAIT! OR IS IT—TRAPAR?!
DON'T TELL ME IT'S—!

BATTLE GROUP 02 DESTROYED...!!

...!!

WHAT THE HELL KIND OF WEAPON CAN...?!

WHOA!

KLIK! KLIK!

THERE IT IS, THE STUFF OF LEGENDS...

THE "SEVENTH SWELL"—!

SO! AWAKENED AT LAST...
WHAT THE...
...HECK WAS...?
!

...DID IT COME FROM *HIM*–?

...OH. RIGHT.

I-IT MEANS TO *WANT*... O-OR TO *NEED*, OR...

THAT IT'S *IM-PORTANT*, OR...

A-AND NOT JUST BETWEEN *PEOPLE*, EITHER, BUT...

!

TAP

IT SEEMS THAT, TO NIRVASH...

...IT'S GOOD THAT YOU'RE HERE.

GULP!

HEY ...

WHADDA THEY CALL YOU, ANYWAY?

"EUREKA."

......!?

LIKE ON THAT COMPUTER SCREEN...?

EUREKA

SO YOU'RE THE ONE WHO AWAKENED NIRVASH, HUH...?

I THANK YOU FOR YOUR ACTIONS... AND YOUR COURAGE.

GLATT

H-HOLLAND ?!

I-I'M RIGHT HERE!!

R-RENTON THURSTON, REPORT-ING FOR DUTY–!

YOU COMING TO JOIN UP WITH US, OR WHAT?

WHAT'S IT GONNA BE?

MY...?

REALLY ?!
THE WAVE I CAUGHT TODAY WAS MAYBE BIGGEST OF ALL...

SAYO-NARA, HOME-TOWN!
SEE YOU LATER, GRAND-PA!
MY AD-VENTURE'S FINALLY BEGUN...
NOT TO MEN-TION–
BEEP
MOON-LIGHT HERE...
SO, ARE YOU DONE YET??
ONLINE
PWOP
MM-HM. ALMOST.
I DIDN'T KNOW YOU HAD A SISTER ...

SEE YOU WHEN YOU GET HOME, THEN...
MAMA!!
...DWAH?

Psalms of Planet Eureka seveN

PLAY

00:20:54

...WHOA.

MURMUR

ULP

MURMUR

MURMUR

...THE LFO OF LEGEND, "NIRVASH"...
...OUR GREATEST OF MILITARY SECRETS, STOLEN, AS YOU KNOW, FROM BENEATH OUR VERY NOSES...
...AND TRACEABLE, TO NO ONE'S SURPRISE...
RUMM

RUMM
HRUMM
...BACK TO OUR GREATEST OF FOES, THOSE ANTI-GOVERNMENT INSURGENTS, THE *GEKKO STATE.*
RUMM
IT'S BEEN THREE DAYS SINCE I CAME ABOARD *MOONLIGHT*, THE SHIP OF MY BOYHOOD DREAMS...
...LEAVING ALL THE BOREDOM AND B.S. OF MY OLD LIFE BEHIND, OR...

...SO I THOUGHT.
KLOMP
YO, RENTON! WHERE'S THAT COFFEE?!
C-COMING RIGHT UP!
KLATTER
MAKE SURE IT'S *BLACK*, LIKE I LIKE IT...
BUT WITH THE FOUR SUGARS, RIGHT?
RIGHT.
HOLLAND, DRIVING FORCE BEHIND *MOONLIGHT*...
HOW COOL IS *HE*-?!
...OR, SO I'D THOUGHT.
SLURRRP
SKRITCH SKRITCH

RENTON-N-N, WHERE'S MY TOWEL...??
C-COMING!
STAGGER
TALHO, THE SHIP'S HELMSMAN...
LOOKING JUST AS GLAMOROUS AS SHE DID IN HER PIN-UP FOR GEKKO STATE'S "RAY=OUT" MAGAZINE...
THA-A-ANK YOU! ♥
HEY! THIS TOWEL IS STILL WET—!!
AND I'M STILL WAITING ON THAT BEER.
MOVE IT!!
SNAPP
F-FORGIVE ME!
...OR, SO I ONCE THOUGHT.
TOUGH TIMES, HUH, KID?
DON'T FORGET TO FINISH THIS REPORT FOR ME.
PWAP
......
LET'S FACE IT...

I MAY AS WELL BE THEIR SERVANT-!
MUCH MORE OF THIS...
...AN' I'LL BE DONE FOR!
NOT THAT I'D CHANGE IT, EVEN IF I COULD.
STAGGER
STAGGER
SIGH
AN' DIDN'T IT LOOK ALL SOFT AND SMUSHY UNDER TALHO'S ...?
WHAT A FUNNY FACE!

EU...
EUREKA!
I-I WASN'T *BETRAYING* YOU...N-NOT IN MY *HEART*, ANYWAY! I...
OR SO I *DID* THINK!
...YUP. THIS IS THE HARDEST PART, ALL RIGHT.
FUNNY FACE.
PINCH
!
......
B-BMP
B-BMP
—OKAY, SO SHE'S A LITTLE WEIRD. STILL...
YOU CAN'T HELP BUT *LOVE* HER, RIGHT?
RIGHT ??
STOMP
STOMP
STOMP

BAH-BOOT!
HAIYAH!!
!
ZWAH
BWAH
DWAH
LINCK!
...MAE-TER!
MAU-RICE!
LAY ANOTHER FINGER ON OUR MAMA AND YOU'RE *HAMBURGER,* GOT IT?!
OOH, HAMBUR-GER. YUM.
.....
YOU HEARD IT...

THE GIRL OF MY DREAMS...
...IS "MAMA" TO THREE OTHER KIDS.
SLUMP
WHY IS IT I CAME HERE, AGAIN...?
HEY! GET OFFA M—
HORSEY RENTON, HORSEY!
GWEHH!
OW-OW-OW-OWW!!
......
BUT, ADMIRAL, WHY—?!

KINDLY REMEMBER, MISTER DOMINIC, THAT HE IS THE *CAUSE* OF OUR CURRENT SITUATION ...
I'VE NO INTENTION OF RE-LEASING HIM FROM IMPRISON-MENT.
BUT, SIR–!

LOOK AT THIS, WILL *YOU?!*
See?
CAN YOU *BELIEVE* THESE *SCRATCH-ES??*

THIS IS NO TIME TO...
!

–*THIS* KITTY, ON THE OTHER HAND, IS A GOOD GIRL...
MEOW
SUCH A CUTIE...

....
THE OTHER CAT–WHAT HAPPENED TO...?

HERE'S THE THING...
I CAN'T *STAND* A STUPID CAT.

...IF YOU'LL EXCUSE ME.

K-TUNK

GRIND

......!

THE THING ABOUT EUREKA...?

SHE MAY NOT LOOK IT, BUT SHE IS 30.

FLUTTA FLUTTA
OH, MATTHIEU. WHO'D *BELIEVE* SUCH A THING?
HIM, FOR STARTERS!
I JUST *LOVE* HAVING A NEW TOY TO PLAY WITH–!
AHA-HA-HAH
HE'LL FIND OUT ABOUT EUREKA AND THE KIDS SOON ENOUGH ...
TILL THEN, LET ME HAVE MY *FUN*, EH, HILDA?
IT SURE ISN'T FOR *ME* TO TELL HIM WHAT HAPPENED WITH–

...SHE'S THERE, AGAIN.
MAMA, OUT TALKING TO NIRVASH.
NICE DRAWERS, MAETER ...
VWIP
HOL-LAND, DON'T BE GROSS!
IF YOU LIKE GRANNY-PANTIES.
YOU'RE THE ONE WHO FLASHED YOUR—!
WONDER WHAT IT IS THEY TALK ABOUT...?
....
GOOD QUES-TION...
WHAT DOES A YOUNG GIRL WHO CAN COAX THE BEST FROM A MACHINE...
...HAVE TO TALK ABOUT WITH THE FIRST LFO DISCOVERED IN THE WORLD?

NO ONE UNDER-STANDS THE MACHINE HEART LIKE HER, THEY SAY...
AND, NO MATTER HOW TRUE OR NOT THAT MAY BE...
...THERE'S NO DISPUTING THAT SHE IS, IN FACT, SPECIAL.
EU-REKA—HEY.
DON'T PLAY SUCH FAVORITES WITH NIRVASH...
MAETER AND THE OTHERS NEED YOUR ATTENTION, TOO.
BE A MOM.
!

...ALL RIGHT.
YAAY!
THERE YOU HAVE IT.
SHE NEVER GETS ANGRY...
...AND SHE NEVER SMILES.
...SOME-THING WRONG?
WELL...
WHY *DID* NIRVASH AWAKEN?
WHY TO ONE SO... INDECISIVE?

"IN-DECI–"? ...AH.

YOU MEAN THE *NO CONFIDENCE* THING.

He is still a kid.

THEN IT'S A *BAD* THING...

HAVING NO CONFIDENCE.

...WELL, YEAH!

HOW CAN YOU BELIEVE IN YOURSELF WITHOUT IT??

... HUH.

IT *COULD* BE THAT IT WASN'T RENTON AT ALL, BUT MERELY **NIRVASH** AT LAST HAVING ALL ITS PARTS...

RENTON MAY IN FACT HAVE NOTHING TO *DO* WITH IT!

*CIF=Compact Interferencer

?
"CIF" ?
TUG
TUG
TUG
IT USES ENEMY *RADAR WAVES* TO CANCEL OUT THE ODD BITS OF TRAPAR EMITTED BY THE COMPACT DRIVE...
See ya!
Compact Inter-Ferencer
WITHOUT THE CIF, WE WOULDN'T BE ABLE TO TRAVEL ABOUT FREELY AND UNDETECTED.

SO THEN IF THAT'S *BROKEN*—!
AN *INTERFERENCE* SENSOR SEEMS TO HAVE SHORTED-OUT...
WOZ IS ALREADY ON IT, BUT WE CAN'T SEEM TO LOCATE THE POINT OF ORIGIN.
NOT TO RUSH OR ANYTHING, BUT 172 SECONDS TILL ARRIVAL OF PATROL BATTALION ...
WHADDYA WANNA DO, HOLLAND?

HNNM ...
LUR-R-RP

IS THE MOON-LIGHT...
...IN DANGER?!

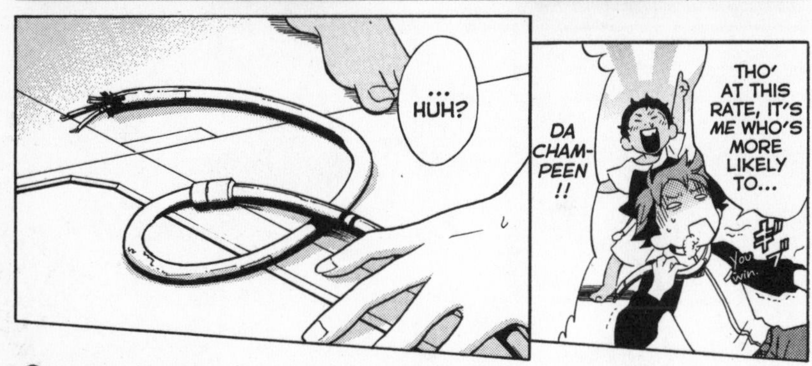
THO' AT THIS RATE, IT'S ME WHO'S MORE LIKELY TO...
DA CHAMPEEN!!
You win.
...HUH?

UM, LINCK...? THIS CABLE— WHERE DID YOU...?
HUH? I DUNNO—IT WAS JUST KINDA STICKIN' OUT!!
WHO DA MAN?!
....
DOOOM

LINCK!
I SHOULD-!!
"I" ...?
"EYE" ...?
"AYE" ...?
DON'T LOOK AT ME-!
Any smarter and they'd be a three-year-old.

RENTON!
EUREKA!
!
YES?

LAUNCH THE NIRVASH.
!!

BUT, HOLLAND!
コポポ GLUG GLUG
CAN IT.
YOU OTHERS'LL SERVE AS A DECOY.
WE NEED YOU TO BUY TIME SO *MOONLIGHT* CAN ESCAPE.
DRAW THE PATROL BATTALION AWAY.
ENOUGH TIME FOR THIS COFFEE TO COOL SHOULD DO IT...

NOW, GO!
G-GOING!

WHAT'S HE THINKING...?
ガリ… GNAW...
THAT CABLE SHOULD TAKE NEXT TO *NO* TIME TO...
ALL FOR ONE, LOUSY PATROL BATTALION?
IF WE LAUNCH NIRVASH, THEY'LL ONLY GO AFTER *IT*, AND...
!

...YOU'RE *TESTING* THEM.

TALHO...

BRING ME SOME SUGAR, HUH?

MAKE IT FOUR.

KLINK

...COFFEE AGAIN, ENSIGN DOMINIC?

THAT CAN'T BE GOOD FOR YOU.

I STARTED DRINKING THE STUFF JUST TO BE *SOCIAL* WITH SOMEONE I... WELL, NOW I CAN'T STOP.

NO, OF COURSE.

AND SO?

THE WHITE LFO WE'VE BEEN SEEKING HAS BEEN FOUND!
RIGHT! THIS IS A PRIORITY MISSION!!
KLATT
LET MOONLIGHT BE...
IT'S NIRVASH THAT WE'RE AFTER-!!
KLATT

RELAX.
RELAX.
RELAX.
B-BMP
ULP
OKAY, SO FINALLY I'M NOT JUST A *SERVANT* ANY MORE, BUT...
B-BMP
B-BMP
PHOO-O-O
HOW DO I KNOW I CAN DO THIS?
B-BMP

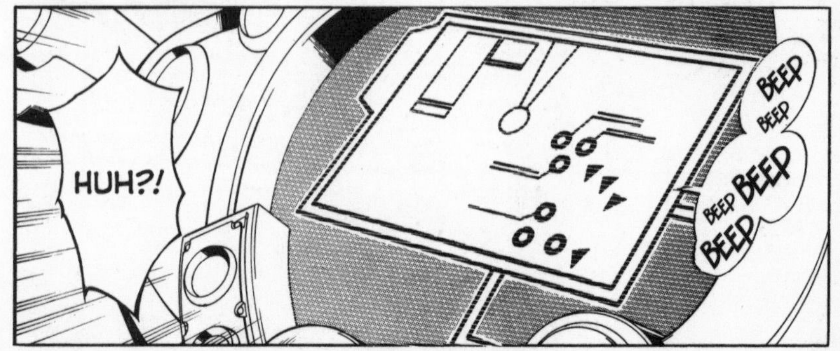

UWAH?!
MORE PATROL BATTALION SHIPS!
DOOSH
DOOSH
ZPOKK
DOOSH
...GEEZ! DON'T WE AT *LEAST* GET A *WARNING*?!
VZOOOM

WHAT'S GOING ON?!
PATROL BATTALION H-25 HERE...
TARGET MANEUVERED INTO POSITION!
EXCELLENT! LEAVE THE REST TO THE SURFACE BATTALION.
THAT VALLEY THEY'RE IN IS *FAMOUS* FOR TRAPAR...
FOR NOT *HAVING* ANY, THAT IS! AND, WITHOUT TRAPAR TO BUOY THEM...
THEY'RE IN FOR A *VERY* HARD LANDING.

SHUDDER
!?
KRACKLE
KRACKLE
KRACKLE
THE *LIFT BOARD'S* LOSING BUOYANCY...
THERE'S NO TRAPAR—!!
WAAAH!!
GWOH
BEEP
HEY.

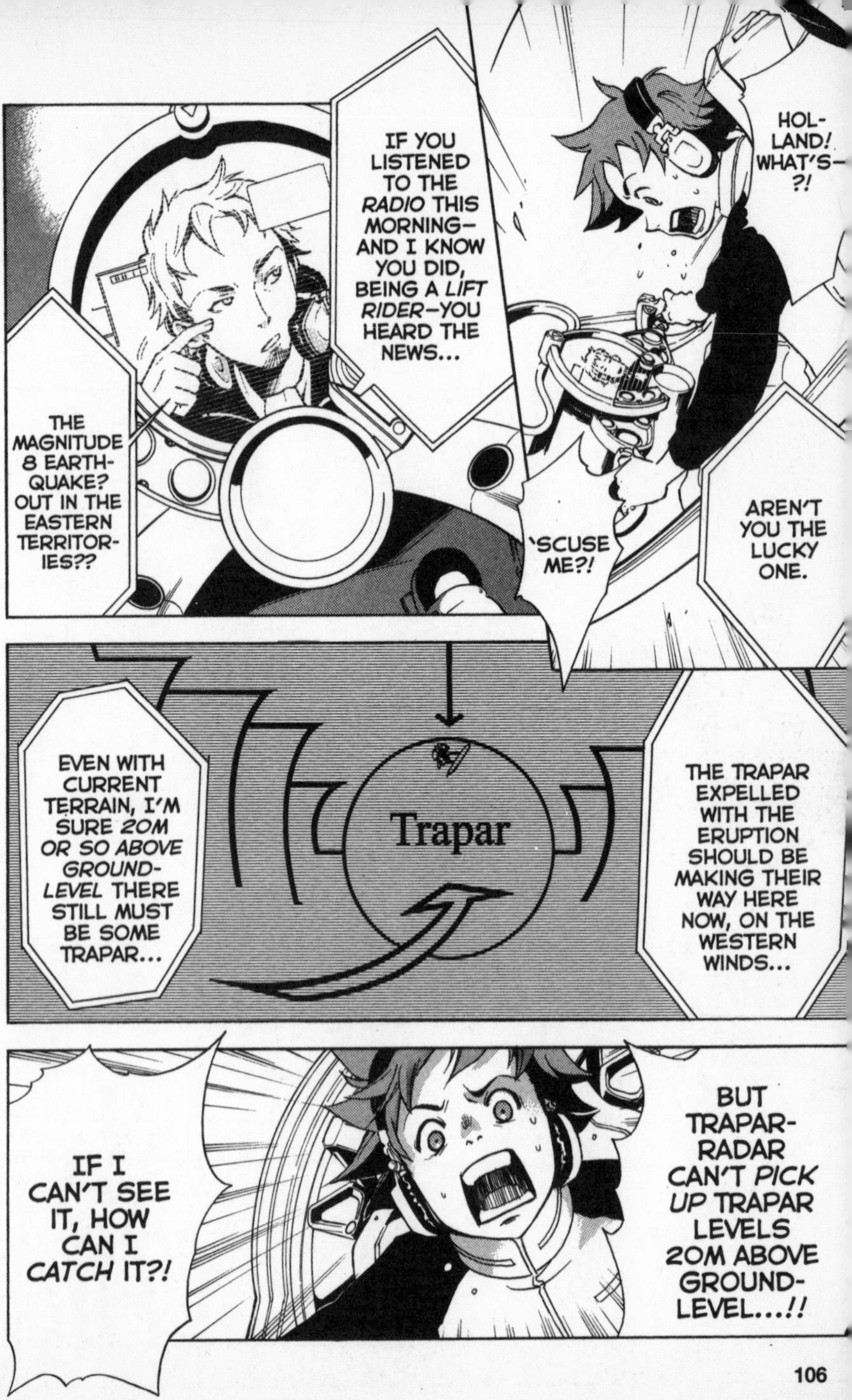

HOL-LAND! WHAT'S—?!

IF YOU LISTENED TO THE *RADIO* THIS MORNING—AND I KNOW *YOU* DID, BEING A *LIFT RIDER*—YOU HEARD THE NEWS...

THE MAGNITUDE 8 EARTH-QUAKE? OUT IN THE EASTERN TERRITOR-IES??

AREN'T YOU THE LUCKY ONE.

'SCUSE ME?!

THE TRAPAR EXPELLED WITH THE ERUPTION SHOULD BE MAKING THEIR WAY HERE NOW, ON THE WESTERN WINDS...

EVEN WITH CURRENT TERRAIN, I'M SURE *20M OR SO ABOVE GROUND-LEVEL* THERE STILL MUST BE SOME TRAPAR...

Trapar

HELL IF I KNOW...
FIGURE IT OUT!
WHAT?!
NOT IN FRONT OF THE WOMEN, HUH KID?
WAIT A... WHAT'RE YOU GONNA *DO*, LET HIM *DIE*?!
HE'S NO GOOD ON *MOONLIGHT* IF HE'S USELESS...
C'MON, ROOKIE... SHOW ME A MIRACLE!!

BUT TRAPAR'S *INVISIBLE* WITHOUT THE RADAR!
I CAN'T EVEN *SEE* IT, NEVER MIND–
GWOSHH
YOU'LL BE FINE.
YOU CAN DO IT.
NIRVASH SAYS THE SAME.
!
BELIEVE IN YOURSELF.
......
HOW CAN I?

HOL-LAND'S ONE THING...
...AND *YOU*, EUREKA, YOU'RE ANOTHER, BUT...
I'M NOT *LIKE* YOU GUYS!
HOW I WAS AT SCHOOL ...
HOW I WAS ON *MOON-LIGHT*...
HOW DO I EXPLAIN?
I...
I JUST CAN'T *DO* THE STUFF YOU DO-!!
I'M SORRY.
THERE'S NOTHING I...
......
RIGHT, THEN.

IF YOU CAN'T BELIEVE IN YOUR-SELF...
...I'LL DO THE BELIEVING *FOR YOU*.
NIRVASH WILL BELIEVE IN *ME*...
...AND *YOU* BELIEVE IN **NIRVASH**, OKAY?
YOU
ME
NIRVASH
YOU SEE HOW THAT WORKS OUT?
....
カン
ポ
DURGHH
UM...
OKAY.

BWAH, HA, HAH ...!
TWIK
!?
...SORRY.
?
WHAT A PAIR, HUH?
GWOHH
SET ANGLE OF APPROACH FOR 22 DEGREES!
SHAFT STABIL-IZED— 71M TO SURFACE!
NOW 53M...
40M ...
29M ...
!?
25M ...
WOHHH
17M...

I CAN SEE IT! THERE'S...
...NO WAY I CAN, BUT I *DO*!
HOWEVER IT *IS* I CAN...
GLINT
I SEE THE TRAPAR!!
I CAN DO THIS!!
HUH?
HWAAHN?!

ZBWOSSH
ALL RIGHT—I CAUGHT IT!
WOBBLE
WHOA, WATCH THE BALANCE!
!
WOBBLE
EUREKA... RIGHT! NO, LEFT!!
ZBOSSH
WATCH OUT FOR THE COWS...
WHOA... WHOA!!
ZBOSSH
!?

ZWOOP
I DID IT!!

!!!
A CUT-BACK DROP TURN—!!

YO, YO... YOU CAN'T *LIFT* LIKE THAT ON AN *LFO*...!!
KLIK
KLIK
Dude!
......
...HA, HA, HAH!
HE NOT ONLY SEES THE TRAPAR, BUT PULLS THAT MOVE...??
WHO'D'VE THUNK IT?!

YOU'RE NOT SO USELESS AFTER ALL...

...ARE YOU, RENTON THURSTON–!!

DIDJA SEE THAT, EUREKA? DIDJA SEE WHAT I DID?!

ぶん PUMP

ぶん PUMP

HOW COOL WAS THAT, HUH? HUH??

AND IT'S ALL THANKS TO YOU, EUREKA! YOU'RE THE BEST!!

...REN-TON?
C'MON, KID, OR THAT *PATROL BATTALION* WILL GET YOU.
I-I'M FINE. IT'S JUST...
N-NOW THAT IT'S OVER, I'M KINDA FEEL-ING... KIND OF...
?
ULP

GLAA-A-A-ARGH-H-H
........!!!

BLACK, AS YOU LIKE IT...
AND WITH...

TIME, IT SEEMS, HAS BECOME TO *MOVE*...

DO YOU KNOW, I'M SO EXCITED, I THINK I MIGHT JUST DANCE A WALTZ...!

Psalms of Planet Eureka seveN

*KLF=Craft Light Fighter, an LFO equipped for combat

SURVIVOR STATUS UNKNOWN ...
KZZT
-ROGER THAT. STAY ALERT AND CONTINUE SEARCH. OVER.
KRUNCH

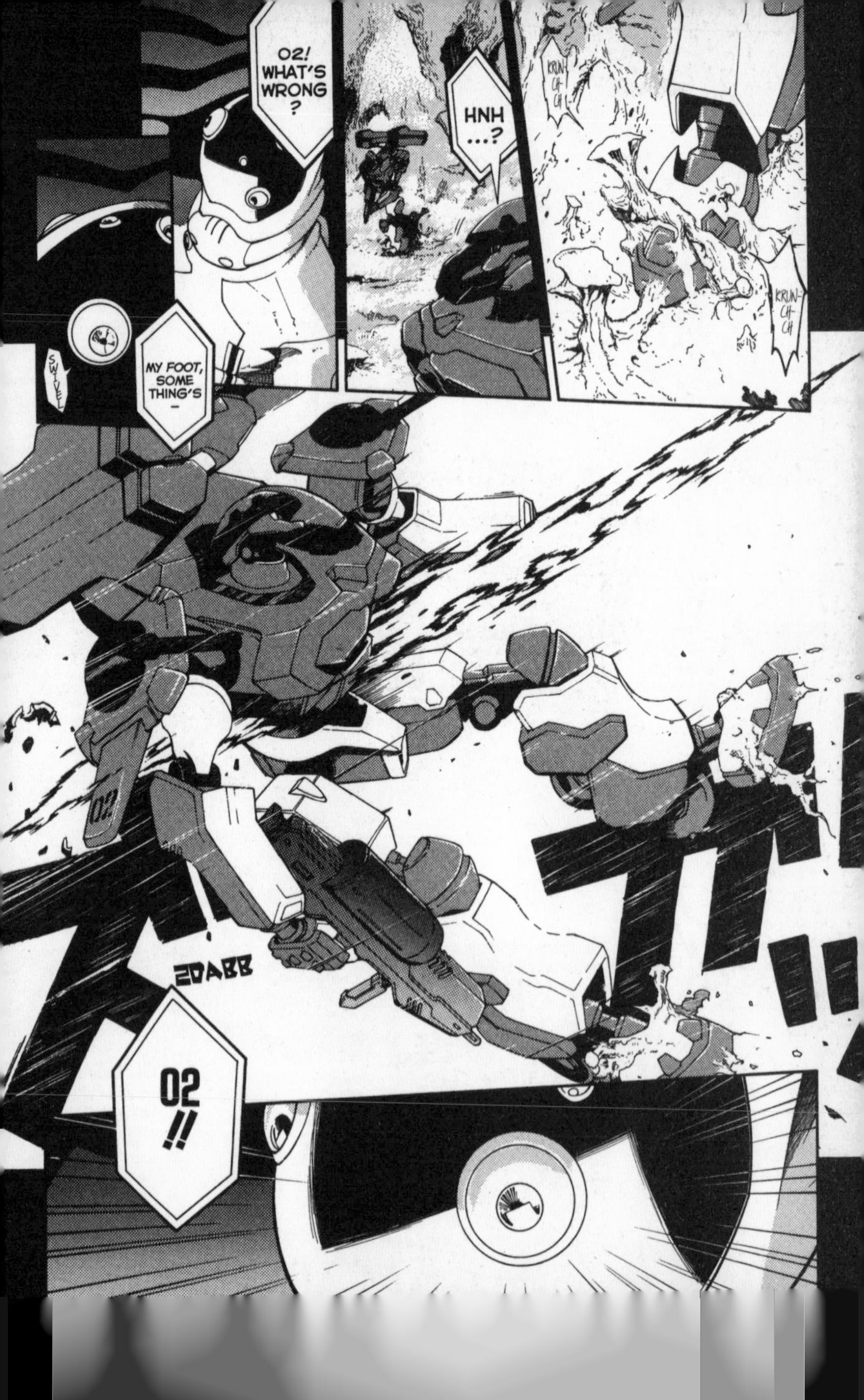
KRUN-CH-CH
KRUN-CH-CH
HNH ...?
02! WHAT'S WRONG ?
SWIVEL
MY FOOT, SOME THING'S —
ZDABB
02 !!

WHAT'S WRONG? REPORT—!!
IT... IT—!
COME IN!!
HEAT SIGNATURES DETECTED...
BEEP
BEEP
BEEP
...MORE THAN ONE—ALL OVER THE PLACE!
UWAHHHH!!!
BLAM
BLAM
BLAM
BLAM
BLAM
BLAM

ZDOOM
ZZT

03 HOLIDAYS IN THE SUN

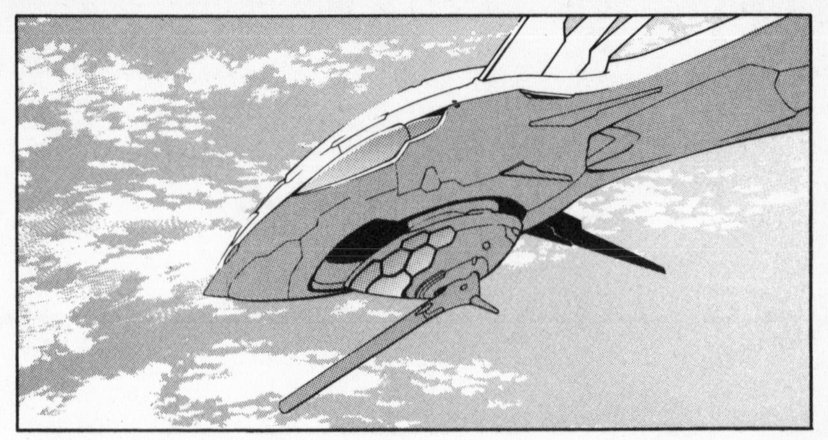

GUR-R-RGLE
DROOOL

NO-O-O-!
ZDOPP!
K-KEEN
!
ZWASH
AH HA HAH
HEY, I'M A GROWING BOY, OKAY?!
REN-TON!
?
HE-E-ERE, KITTY-KITTY.
PEEL
PLOP

GAH!!
PLAP
TH-THE LAST CRO-QUETTE...
HEY...
IF YOU GUYS DON'T WANNA EAT IT, I WILL.
むぐ
CHOMP

HAP-YOU DIDN'T-!
TELL ME HE DIDN'T JUST EAT THAT OFF THE FLOOR.
HE'S MADE OF STERNER STUFF THAN US, OUR SUB-LEADER...
"Three-second rule," huh...?

I'M HUN-N-NGRY-!
GURGLE
EUR-EUREKA'S UNDIES...
EURE-KA'S-!!
GURGLE
FOOD SUPPLIES ARE RUNNING LOW ON *MOONLIGHT* AT THE MOMENT...

MOSTLY THIS IS DUE TO THE SHEER SIZE OF THE CREW...
WOULD YOU BELIEVE THERE'S 18 OF US?!
FOOD—AND EVERYTHING ELSE, FOR THAT MATTER—TENDS TO DISAPPEAR ALMOST IMMEDIATELY ...
KLATTA

IF NOTHING ELSE, WE NEED VEGET-ABLES AND RICE...
CIGAR-MAN'S LATEST LP, MAN!
CIGARMAN
WAX FOR LIFT BOARDS ...
20 NEW TOOTH-BRUSHES !
I SAW JUST THE CUTEST RING THE OTHER DAY... ♡
WE NEED FILM...
AND COFFEE.
AN-N-ND...
チャ
CH-CHANG
...YOU WANT ME TO BUY ALL THAT WITH ONLY THIS...?

IT'S NOT ENOUGH!!
BUT IT'S ALL THE MONEY WE HAVE...
YOU'RE THE PRO-CUREMENT OFFICER; *YOU* FIGURE IT OUT.
...WHY DON'T WE JUST DO SOME *WORK*, OR–?
I AM!
NEXT ISSUE OF "RAY=OUT," HEH-LOH!
ray=out
SO TALHO'S ON THE COVER AGAIN, HUH?
WASN'T SHE ON THE *LAST* ONE, TOO...?
IF SHE'S NOT, IT WON'T SELL...
IT WON'T SELL *ANYWAY*, BUT...
IT *IS* JUST A HOBBY-MAG–GIVE US A
....
WELL, WHAT ABOUT *OTHER* WORK, THEN?
WE COULD START OUR OWN *DELIVERY SERVICE*, OR...

—NAH.

TODAY ...

...WE GOT SOMETHIN' *WAY* MORE IMPORTANT TO DO.

SO MANY PEOPLE TODAY, OUT AND ABOUT...
YEAH, AND US WITH SO LITTLE CASH...
Aha. Aha-hah...
WOO
WOO
YAAY
YAAY
THEY FIGHT FOR SCRAPS OF FOOD AND WON'T LIFT A FINGER TO SAVE THEMSELVES...
"GEKKO STATE," HUH? MORE LIKE WELFARE STATE, IF YOU ASK ME...
Puh-leeze...
THERE MUST BE SOMETHING TO...
WA-A-AIT A SEC!

COULD IT BE...
...THEY'VE SET US UP ON OUR FIRST DATE–?!
SMACKAH!
DON'T YOU THINK NASTY THOUGHTS ABOUT OUR MAMA–!
ずぅぅん
ZWOOOM
...C-COMPLETE WITH THREE KIDS.
LOOKS DELICIOUS...
OOH!
Doesn't it?!
FROM THE MOST RECENT ISSUE OF "MANLY HORIZONS"...
"CHERRY LOVERS ARE GREAT KISSERS."
DUM-DUM-DUM!
男の水平線

HYAAAAAH!
パターン!
SLAM!
?
LOOK, MAMA, LOOK!
...SHE'S SO CUTE.
LET'S SEE. "A RED DRESS MEANS SHE–"
ペラッ
FLIP

男の水平線 vol.24
!!
LOOK— BALLOONS! BALLOONS!!
BETTER NOT GET MY HOPES UP.
REF BOARD MEET
!
A LIFT TOURNA-MENT—!
I SURE WISH *I* COULD LIFT RIGHT N—
FLUTTA
HEY, EUREKA... I BET YOU'VE SEEN HOL-LAND AND THE GUYS LIFT *PLENTY* OF TIMES, HUH?
SURE.

SO HOW GOOD ARE THEY?!
DO THEY HAVE ANY SPECIAL STANCE, OR...?
THEY DON'T *HANG* ON THEIR CUT-BACKS, DO THEY?
CAN THEY DO A FULL 360°, ALL THE WAY 'ROUND??
EURE-KA?
... HUH.
THAT BOARD...
POOR THING.
IT'S BEEN SO MIS-TREATED.
YOU'RE RIGHT— IT'S FALLING APART.
NO ONE WHO TREATS A LIFT BOARD LIKE THIS CAN BE ANY GOOD AT...
STEP

...GO ON.

WE'RE LISTENIN'.

NNRGH!
SH-SHOWS WHAT YOU KNOW!
I-I'M A MEMBER OF GEKKO STATE, AND—
SNORT
やははははは
BWAH HA HA HA HAH
WAH-HA-HAH! YEAH SURE, KID—I BET!
YEAH! A MEMBER OF GEKO STATE *DAYCARE*, MAYBE!!
Y-YOU THINK I'M KIDDING?!
"GEKKO STATE," HUH...?

WHAT *ABOUT* THOSE SECOND-RATE LIFTERS...?

...YEAH. *THEM.*

GRRR

"SECOND-RATE"—?!

.....
I-I HAVEN'T REALLY...
...NO, HUH? HA, HA, HA.
WHAT DO *YOU* KNOW?!
I'D TELL YOU OFF, BUT–
I'VE SEEN HIM.
WHEN THEY LIFT, HOLLAND AND THE OTHERS...
...REALLY "LIVE IN THE MOMENT."
.....?
HWAH?
CHICK'S TOTALLY *GONE,* MAN...
LET'S GET OUTTA HERE.
......
FRUIT
ME.

HEY MISTER! YOU GOT A **BOOGER** ON YOUR NOSE.

DUM-DUM-DUMM!

Booger!

Booger!

DWUMP
ZDOMP
!?
ZDOMP
ZDOMP
HAFF
HAFF
RENTON. WHAT TOOK YOU SO LONG...?
...UM...
WHAT HAPPENED TO YOUR FACE–?!

HORRAND, ROOK—!!
RIFT CONTEST! WE GOTTA!!
second Edition
TWO MILLION IN PRIZE MONEY!!
TWO BIRDS, ONE STONE ...
OUR FOOD *AND* MONEY PROB-LEMS—!
......
DWAH?
OHHH, *I* GET IT...
THE GUYS WHO *DID* THAT TO YOU— YOU WANNA SHOW 'EM UP, HUH?
IRK!
N-NOT NECES-SARILY...!
WE MAKE IT A POINT *NEVER* TO LIFT FOR MONEY...
BESIDES, WITH THE TRAPAR SO THIN 'CAUSE OF SO MANY PEOPLE, WHAT *FUN* WOULD IT BE?
...OH.

IF THAT'S SO, WHEN *DO* THEY...?

I'VE YET TO SEE HOLLAND OR EVEN ANY OF THE OTHERS *OUT* THERE.

GEKKO STATE...

THE GROUP I KEPT *IDOLIZING* FOR SO LONG...

SWOOP...

RI-I-I-P

LIKE I ALREADY SAID, WE GOT SOMETHING GOING ON TODAY.
......
I'M SORRY.
—THEN LET'S GET GOING.

LET'S CATCH SOME WAVES WHILE THEY'RE STILL HOT.
AW-W-W, YEAH!
WHILE THEY'RE *HOT*, MAN-!
...HUH?
VRUM
VRUM

WHAT'S WITH THIS BIG, HUGE, GAPING...?
WHAT, THEY DIDN'T TELL YOU?!
OH, HOLLAND—YOU MEANIE!
NOW I GET IT...
Aha!
SO THAT'S WHY THE KID WAS TRYIN' TO SIGN US ALL UP.
STEP
FUN'S BEST WHEN SAVED FOR LAST.

HERE.
CATCH
!
MY LIFT BOARD–!
Y' DON'T MEAN...
WE'RE AT A– ?!
VRUM
VRUM
VRUM
VRUM
RIGHT ON TIME...
VRUM
VRUM
VRUM
3...
...2
VRUM
VRUM
VRUM
VRUM
1
VRUM

VRUMMMMMM

LET'S GO!!

A TRAPAR ERUPTION-!!
ON WHAT WIND, THOUGH?!
HOW 'BOUT IT, RENTON! BET YOU NEVER CAUGHT ONE THIS BIG-!!
VRUMMM
THAT'S NOT A WAVE, THAT'S A TSUNA-
AN' I'M S'PPOSED TO RIDE IT??
VRUMMM
ZROOM

ZWAHH
WAH!
SWOOM
!

NOW *THIS*...
...*THIS* IS THE REAL GEKKO STATE—NOT THE ONE IN "RAY=OUT."
EVERYTHING *ELSE* GOES AWAY, AND...
...YOU JUST...

...LIVE IN THE MOMENT.
WHOA!
ZLOOP

HOH!

HAH!

フラ
FLAIL

フラ
FLAIL

フラ
FLAIL

TOH!

ビターン
ZDUMP

......

WAIT, WAIT— SO, ON AN LFO, HE *CAN* LIFT...

...WHILE, ON AN ACTUAL LIFT *BOARD*, HE CAN'T??

グサ
STAB

グサ
STAB

THEY'RE JUST TEASING— DON'T LET IT GET TO YOU.

Ha ha ha

KINDA HURTS THE *IMAGE*, THOUGH, HUH?

グサ
STAB

AT LEAST...
...I DIDN'T SCRATCH MY BOARD.
どよーん
GLOOOM
You just pay them no never-mind...
... EUREKA?
......
STARE
TO WORRY ABOUT YOUR BOARD LIKE THAT...
...TAKES A KIND HEART.

LAH-H-H!
DON'T YOU BE TRICKED BY HIM, MAMA!
THIS IS THE GUY WHO THREW UP IN FRONT OF YOU, REMEMBER?!
HEH-LOH, STILL HERE!!
ZBOMP
WAH, HA, HAH...!
I'M GLAD YOU'RE AMUSED.

HE'S SOMETHIN', THAT KID...
LIGHTS UP THE ROOM, JUST TO LOOK AT 'IM.
AND IT DOESN'T HURT, HIS BEING THE SON OF *ADROCK*...
HE USED TO SAY HE COULD SEE TRAPAR, TOO.
HOLLAND.
SO IT'S NO LONGER JUST ME AND EUREKA...
...BUT NOW *YOU'RE* DRAGGING *HIM* INTO THIS, TOO?

DON'T TELL ME YOU'RE TRYING TO SAVE THE WORLD...
...LIKE HE ONCE TRIED TO DO--?
ENOUGH.
ME AN' HIM...
WE'RE NOTHING ALIKE.

DEWEY AND ME ARE NOTHING ALIKE.
....
...I WONDER.

–DEWEY NOVAK! ARE YOU LISTENING?!
...HUH?
OH, UH... SORRY.

AUGUST THOUGH THE WORDS OF THIS TRIUMVIRATE MAY BE...

...I SOMEHOW FIND THE WHITE WALLS OF *MY PRISON* MORE INTEREST-ING.

IN FOLLOWING ADROCK'S PLAN...
...I AM, AFTER ALL, THE ONLY ONE WHO CAN SAVE THIS WORLD.
ZROOM
HERE ...
...CON-FIRMATION THAT, TODAY, ANOTHER BATTALION WAS LOST.

YOU SUGGEST WE'VE LAIN IDLE, DONE NOTHING??
...NO.
BUT WE SHALL HEAR ABOUT IT FROM *MEDEA*, NONETHE-LESS.
THEN WHAT *DO* YOU SUGGEST?!

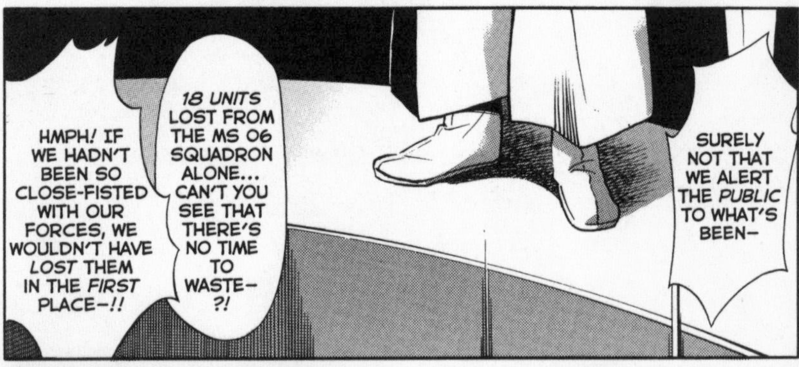
SURELY NOT THAT WE ALERT THE *PUBLIC* TO WHAT'S BEEN-
18 UNITS LOST FROM THE MS 06 SQUADRON ALONE... CAN'T YOU SEE THAT THERE'S NO TIME TO WASTE-?!
HMPH! IF WE HADN'T BEEN SO CLOSE-FISTED WITH OUR FORCES, WE WOULDN'T HAVE *LOST* THEM IN THE *FIRST* PLACE-!!

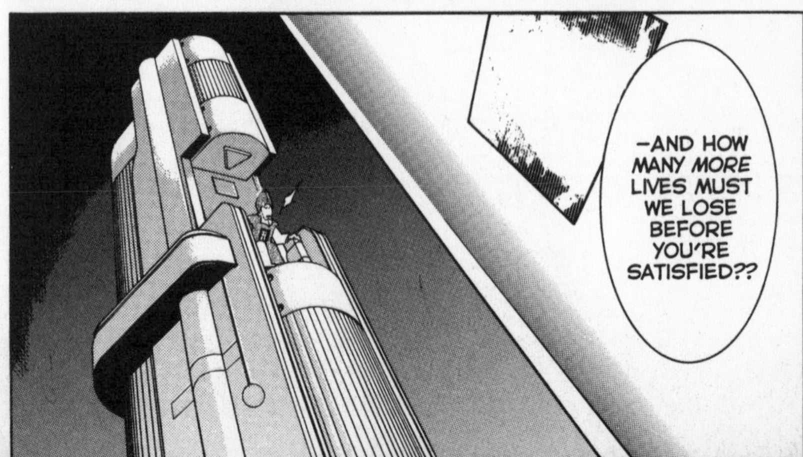
-AND HOW MANY *MORE* LIVES MUST WE LOSE BEFORE YOU'RE SATISFIED??

THE OLD WAYS HAVE THEIR PLACE, BUT THIS BATTLE AGAINST *THEM* IS DIFFERENT!
THEY FIGHT ON *SHEER INSTINCT*, AND THAT ALONE...
...AS A MOTH, DRAWN TO THE FLAME.
!?
FOR IT *IS* WONDROUS, IS IT NOT...?
NOT ONLY HAVE THEY NOT EVOLVED, THEY'RE NOT EVEN *AWAKENED*—!

THEY—THE CORALIANS
!!
TO BE CONTINUED...

EUREKA DOES THE LAUNDRY

END-OF-VOLUME BONUS MANGA

Kataoka Jinsei & Kond_ Kazuma

WHO LEFT THAT IN THE MIDDLE OF THE FLOOR?!
STUB
SHOULD WE TRY AND WORK AROUND HIM...?
I GUESS.
ZZZZ...

EX-SCUSE ME.
THE HELL-?!
♪

ワー YAAY
ワー YAAY
ゴロ ROLL
ゴロ ROLL
Zzz...

MORN-ING.
OH HEY, EUREKA. G'MORN-ING.
REN-TON...? WAKE UP.
...SETTLE

AFTER RENTON'S THRILLING EXPLOITS IN EPISODE 7 OF THE ANIME SERIES, COMMEMORATIVE SPORTS-JACKET FEVER INFECTS MOONLIGHT–!
"Previously, on Eureka seveN..."
WHADDYA THINK, BABY? AM I HOT, OR NOT?
AAAYYYY!
どーん
GLOOOM
WORDS FAIL ME.

HONEST TO GOOD-NESS DOGGIE, YOU'RE THE ABSOLUTE ULTIMATE!
SWOON
AW, DON'T BE SILLY, GIDGET ...
I'M SURE I'M NOT THAT ULTIMATE.
Next to ultimate, maybe.

They do offer a greater range of movement.
Hee!
They do?
DRAG DRAG
......
... YOU'RE NOT GONNA WEAR THAT?
...WHILE OTHERS OUGHT NOT EVEN TRY.

A NEW TOY FOR NIRVASH

TO BE CONTINUED...?

:character & story

片岡人生 jinsei kataoka

Thanks to you all, the tuna haul this year's been great.

My first job—my first *tankoubon*—there've been so many firsts, my head was really starting to swim. Soon, though, I hope, I'll be able to look back....

The truth is, I am having fun. Thanks go out to Most Excellent Editor "M" (he of the phrase, "Don't be ridiculous") for giving me this most amazing opportunity. I'd like to thank the folks at BONES, Director Ky_da, Yoshida Ken'ichi, and everyone else on the anime staff; thanks also go out to those who helped me with this manga, that grand S.O.B. who gave me all that encouragement and, last but not least, you—the one holding this book in your hands.

postscript

First of all, thanks for your purchase! Somehow, an entire volume of this book—which started with a simple question ("I don't suppose you'd wanna draw some robots?")—has managed to come together, despite all the laughing, the celebrating, the falling-down, the getting-mad, and the falling-down once more.

Director Kyouda, Yoshida Ken'ichi, the staff of BONES, Editor "M" and, of course, Kataoka Jinsei (who helped me put this book together)...all of them have helped me to come this far and I hope, with their continued support, to go pedal-to-the-metal all the way to the end.

近藤 一馬 kazuma kondou

:robots & color & more

thanks

Ekaki Uta
Saiyatani Ryouichi
Nobe Takako
Higuchi Akihiko
Katsura Asuka
Toudou Akito
Tomi'i Masako

special thanks

Takimoto Akihisa

THINGS I WANTED TO KNOW
THINGS I **NEVER** WANTED TO KNOW

N E X T

Psalms of Planet Eureka seveN

Their pursuit of *Moonlight* stepped up and with no choice but to reinstate Dewey after an attack by the mysterious Coralians, the military forces Holland and the others to make an abrupt landing... smack in the middle of the town where certain, terrible acts have been committed. Drama builds as Renton learns more about Eureka's hidden past....

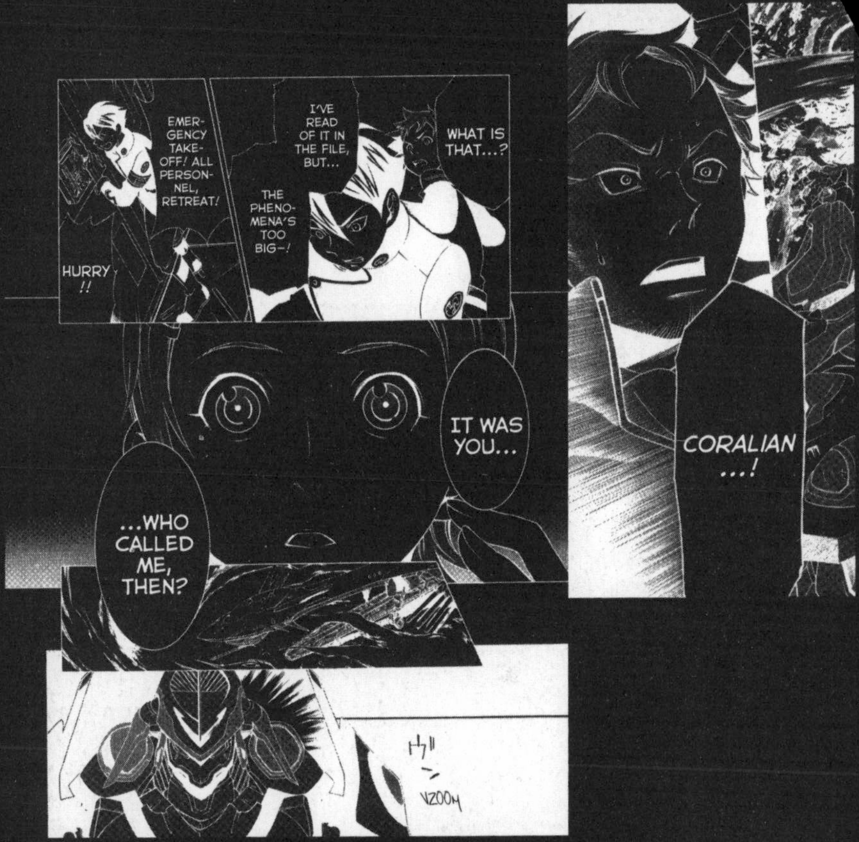

ALL I KNOW IS, I WANNA SAVE EUREKA.

Volume2 coming soon......

YOU ARE READING IN THE WRONG DIRECTION!

STOP

MANGA READS RIGHT TO LEFT, BACK TO FRONT,

SO FLIP THIS BOOK OVER AND ENJOY!

Psalms of Planets Eureka seveN

Volume 1

CONTENTS

ORIGINAL STORY
Bones
STORY AND ART
Jinsei Kataoka & Kazuma Kondou
ORIGINAL BOOK DESIGN
Tsuyoshi Kusano

ENGLISH PRODUCTION CREDITS

TRANSLATION	Toshifumi Yoshida
ADAPTOR	T. Ledoux
LETTERING	Fawn Lau
COVER DESIGN	Kit Loose
EDITOR	Robert Place Napton
COORDINATOR	Rika Davis
PUBLISHER	Ken Iyadomi

Published in the United States
by Bandai Entertainment, Inc.

Regular Edition
ISBN-13: 978-1-59409-664-8
ISBN-10: 1-59409-664-3

Special Edition
ISBN-13: 978-1-59409-665-5
ISBN-10: 1-59409-665-1

Printed in Canada
First Bandai printing: April 2006

10 9 8 7 6 5 4 3 2 1

GEKKOSTATE